# THE TRUMPET

## and other poems

*from*

## East Africa

by

**Mugumya Amooti, R.**

with illustrations by

**P.L. Sanjeewani Gunathilaka**

and more

# EAST AFRICA

I would wish to express my deeply felt gratitude to my young brother Richard Turyamwesimira and my friend Dr. Josephine Tuvuzimpundu for their encouragement throughout my writing career. Their infallible support which comes in different forms has seen me through many storms. Without them, it is probable, that I wouldn't be proud of the fifty or so book titles on my name, so far.

For this particular publication, I humbly acknowledge the hand of Mr. Augustin Ndayizeye who introduced me to Full Media Services.

Finally, I also wish to express my deeply felt gratitude to the editorial board of Full Media Services for perusing my manuscript and recommending it for publication. Similarly, Mr. Philip Weinholtz also deserves a bounty of flesh flowers for taking my manuscript through the tiresome processes of reviewing, editing, designing, and resource allocation to ensure it reaches the publication stage.

**Mugumya Amooti, R.**

For the New Millennium African Patriots robbed of their rightly won political mandate. You may never ascend to political power, but your sacrifice isn't in vain.

There are many, but my mind is particularly on The Right Hon Raila Odinga of Kenya and The Right Hon Morgan Tsvangirai (RIP) of Zimbabwe. The Trumpet roars for the architects of injustice.

# TABLE OF CONTENTS

# POLITICS & GOVERNANCE IN AFRICA

# THE TRUMPET

And your mind wonders –
For whom the trumpet blows!
The trumpet blows for us all.
The trumpet blows for the High and Low,
It blows for both physical and mystical existences!

The trumpet blows loud, though as if the
Majority are in slumber!
Majority of the power-drunken,
Majority of our squinted eye Judges,
Majority of the gun-wielding rulers,
Majority of our boot-leaking power brokers,
All in slumber, and the trumpet blows on.
The trumpet blows thus:

To the power-drunken;
To the squinted-eye Judge,
Justice isn't only meant for the mighty but even the
wretched of the earth -
Be reminded of the call;
The call for fairness.
To the gun-wielding ruler;
Reserve the precious trigger for terrorists
Not justice seeking petitioners.
To the boot-leaking power-brokers;
No permanent friendship in politics.

To us all, the trumpet blows thus:
Col Gaddafi mutilated articles of the Constitution
But was eluded by the eternal ruler!
You will fluke an election victory
But not Statesmanship;
You will imprison an opponent
But not his ideas, and
You will kill the body
But not the soul!
The mountain crashing trumpet oozing out
the ultimate blow, thus:
You will harvest what you sow, and

*"Those who live by the sword will die*
*By the sword"*

# INDEPENDENCE

Colorful celebrations commemorating:
Four decades since the
Fall of Union Jack and self-rule.
Adieu to colonial and dictatorial rule,
Free from imposed leadership,
Free from want and misery
Zee to Western values!
Free to enlist in a single party,
Party condemned to a single leader,
Leader of unquestionable powers,
Powers handed down from above.
Parliamentary and presidential polls on,
The closed-thinker freedom fighter free, but
The open-thinker freedom fighter never eligible!
Patriotic peasants just destined to vote,
Vote the choice of the army,
Army of the party,
Party of the individual head,
Head of the nation.
On Independence Day, the head lists achievements:

Higher GDP figures, Health, Education, security
and prosperity for all.
Endless speech in self-praise,
English was the medium, as
Three-piece clad and bribe-bulged belly cabinet ministers clap;
The cabinet tethered on the presidential will.
Far south - displaced citizens starve,
As amputated opposition sympathizers limp.
Independence, and the independence struggle!
Maybe, it was worth the effort, the drums.

# THE BATTLE OF MEANINGS

### For Dr. Kizza Besigye

There is a man behind the bars of truth,
The silence of truth has ushered
Him into the corridors of hell;
His skeleton crawls towards a cemetery,
*Kayafa* labels his fate a price of justice!
The Nation is undergoing a test of meanings,
*Kayafa's* conscience is also on a test of meanings,
Different classes, same battle-field:

The battle of meanings,
The meaning of democracy, freedom, justice, and truth.
Cursed be these riddling ambiguities,
Ambiguities that have for generations
riddled distinguished professors!

# A PRAYER TO MANDELA

Dear our Nelson Mandela,
The Giant of Generations,
The beaming light of Planets:
Your name, your deeds and universality traversed
the universe,
Your graceful gesture of guidance shone upon
the universe.
Your dream for equality
Knew neither creed nor continent but humanity,
Just called upon for equality,
Neither White domination nor Black domination:
Your sacrifice for South Africa,
Your hand upon Burundi,
Your voice for Palestine,
Pronounced your prime dream of unity

in diversity.
Born a Black in Qunu of South Africa
But your values down your century on earth
Morphoised you into a global citizen and leader,
Before your departure into the dread but sacred planet,
You had ascended to the highest summit of global majesty:

One of the few world icons,
The only secular soul ascending to sainthood alive!
The only president who quit presidency but forever
presided over seven billion hearts!
You flew over to the planet of finality,
Yet your domineering image towers over horizons!

We can see you seated in the sacred planet,
The planet that knows no diversity but universality,
The planet of finality.
The echoes of the drums at your landing
Mopped our tear-drenched hearts,
Replenished our cap of hope,
The hope for your endless vacation.
The stampede of souls scrambling to catch sight of
Your arrival sent us rock-melting earthquakes,
The thunderous salute of angels to usher you in
cleansed us of sadness.

In the last quarter of your century on earth,
Every living soul offered you a hand of friendship,
Everybody cherished your leadership;
As it were on earth, so it will ever be -
We thus see all souls in the sacred planet crave
for your leadership;
As you never knew self-pity,
Your acceptance should be unconditional.
Should African presidents on that sacred planet
Wish to crown you their permanent patron,
As they must indeed,

Please accept the offer unconditionally.
In constituting the Executive of a black council:
Say nay to Idi Amin of Uganda,
Say nay to Jean-Bedel Bokassa of Central Africa,
Say nay to Sani Abacha of Nigeria,
For you could never taste a dish of human blood.
Send the trio and the ilk back to cleanse Africa
of human butcheries.

Say nay to Alhaji Omar Bongo of Gabon,
Say nay to Etienne Eyadema of Togo
For you desisted the temptation of grooming
either Makaziwe Mandela or Zindziswa Mandela
into a political heir,
Send the duo and their ilk back to cleanse Africa
of modern monarchism.
Say nay to Sese Seko Mobutu of Zaire,
Say nay to Juvenal Habyarimana of Rwanda,
Say nay to Kamuzu Banda of Malawi,
Say nay to Col. Gaddafi of Libya,
For you never cherished life presidency,
Send the quantum and their ilk back to cleanse
Africa of life-presidency.

To constitute a fair executive for fairness's sake:
Say yah to Leopold Sedar Senghor of Senegal,
Say yah to Kwame Krumah of Ghana,
Say yah to Julius Nyerere of Tanzania,
Say yah to Seretse Khama of Botswana,
Say yah to Patrice Lumumba of Zaire,
Say yah to Thomas Sankara of Burkina Faso,
Say yah to Seretse Khama of Botswana,
For their call was your call,
their cause was your cause,
their struggle was your struggle -
The people's struggle.
They sacrificed for sovereignty,

They never struggled for self-service but humanity.

Nelson Mandela,
The fallen Mvule tree forever towering over
The tropics and the Amazon,
The sun forever illuminating planets;
The Reviried legend in whose honour
The United States of America shook hands with
The Federal Republic of Cuba!
The retired president forever presiding over
Nations and Kingdoms.

# FAITH
## &
# RELIGION

# GOD

God created man,
Blessed and challenged him to work and conquer
the world.

Man thus acted accordingly -
He erected the tower of Babylon, but
God Himself blew it down!
He erected skyscrapers,
But Earthquakes floored them often;
A ruler captured power,
Masses smoked him out of the throne;
Patriots instituted a nation,
A gluttonic ruler demolished the constitution
to entrench a monarchy;
As a farmer hoped for a bumper harvest,
Swarms of locusts filed forth to prune for him!

Century in, Century out,
Set-backs trailed man's effort, and

Millennia down the road,
Mankind looks forward to conquering the world!
Just like a black ant trying to kick the sky,
Man charges at God demanding to know
the essence of entwining:
Shine and rain,
Hope and despair,
Joy and sorrow,
Ambition and frustration,
Life and death!
Smilingly, God retorted:
How wise of you was it to forget that,
The world is an inter-section of life, and
Life is an everlasting battle?

# OF MODERN TRENDS

All over Kigali City now,
We all sing of new life:
the New life Night-club, and
the New life Christ's Chapel -
Rubbing shoulders and cutting an image of
Identical twins!
Resident on the same flat,
Sharing the arena and flower;
Sky-high and high life melody-
A shared opium to lure their faithful's;
An appropriator shared, too:
An opportune ploy to tap optimal returns.

# PASSAGE OF THE CROSS

Crowds crowded the streets,
Like sky clouds, the crowds roved the streets
On the biblical Good Friday.
The crowds brandished the cross in
Commemoration of His crucifixion,
Crucified that the crowds may access abundant:
Life, love, peace, and harmony.
Yes, the Passage of the Cross to dramatize
Commitment to the commandments!

Cassocks led the crowds,
The cassocks committed not to the call but a vocation!
The crowds harbored worldly hearts:
A beauty show and an exhibition of newly acquired attire!

On converging at Christ, the King,
Testimonies about the day's walk thronged in:
Pauline pitched Peter's man,
A pick pocket searched Sarah's skirts,
James dipped his hand into Jane's bra.

A duo in the match hatched a murder plan,
A trio struck a robbery racket,
Many others sighed for worldly wealth,
Maybe, the match marked a betrayal!
Whatever, would He smile or scream on resurrection?

# MATERIALISM
# &
# MORALITY

# LABOUR DAY
# CELEBRATIONS

In Royale Regence gardens,
The haggard hungry looking
Human shells filled the gardens;
Ears cocked, maybe, He could hint on the issue-
Their salary accounts on the verge of closure;
For four months not even, a coin had been wired thereon!

Their generous employer never delegated,
A man so lavish with words,
But stringent with cash transfers:
'For all your sacrifice and dedication,
I dedicate Sky-Height Estates to you.
For it's owed to your four months' salary arrears.
Today is Labour Day; let's celebrate our grand achievements.'
The generous employer dipped them into drums of
Guinness, Bell lager…
He soaked the rest with cans of spirits,
Spirits and wines of all tribes.
To fill their hallowed narrow bellies,
He subjected each to a seasoned carcass of Turkey, and
That was just an appetizer!

Don Williams, Ken Rodgers…shafted the walls,
The walls seemed to tilt with waves,
Sent them tossing on the floor for a desert.
With spirits up, they descended on the cold spirits;
Eviction notices owed to salary arrears off their memory -
They ruptured with praise songs upon a generous employer.

With booze and buzz,
Twist and waltz,
Their heads twisted onto concrete walls.
Meanwhile, their generous employer still on his bottled water,
Flashed his teeth, bouts of beams abound,
"Victory ever with us the victors –conquerors of human brain,"
He leaped high in the air.

Two months later their accounts were credited,
"Full pay", the pay-slip assured them,
Not six months but four,
For they had walloped two in lieu of Labour day celebration.

# SALARY EARNER'S REFLECTIONS

My schedule is akin of a normal heart beat,
My days are so crowded,
My hours are so few,
So little time and
So much to do, but
My take-home is a molecule!
My freedom is let out for a beggar's dish,
My will is hurled out by whirlwinds of a slave driver.
Forever counting days, counting down days of the month!
Forever obedient, but disobedient to myself, though.

Day in, day out,
Tethered in the slighted service,
Suffocating under a starved family,
Forever slouching in stunted progress,
Scorning God's vision of unalienable entitlement,
The vision of a broad thinker,
A thinker who wouldn't shovel any talent.

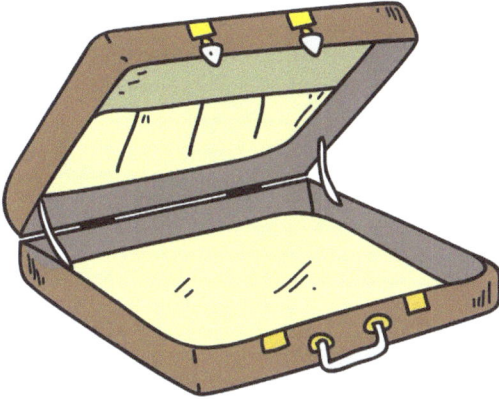

# MAN'S DIALOGUE WITH GOD

As the man lay on his deathbed,
He could only hear Lord's voice,
Saying:

'Son, it's time to go!'
'Now? So soon my Lord, and most of
my plans unaccomplished!'

Drawing a suitcase closer to the man,
God said:

'I'm sorry your time is up; board and we go.'
'What do you have in that suitcase?' asked the man.
'Your belongings', God answered.
Excitedly, 'my belongings?', the man cheered up.
'You mean my property - my suits, my money?'
'No, those were not yours, they belonged to the earth.'
'Is it my power and my ambitions?'
'No, those belonged to Time.'
'Is it my family and friends?'
'No, those belonged to the Path.'
'Is it my wife and my son?'

*'No, those belonged to your heart!'*
*'Is it my nation and my subjects?'*
*'No, they belonged the countrymen!'*
*'Is it my body and my beauty?'*
*'No, those belonged to the dust!'*
*'At least it is my soul.'*
*'Not at all, that one is Mine!'*

Opening the suitcase, the man realized it was empty:

*'My Lord, you mean to say j had nothing*
*and labored in vain?'*

Happy with the man's realization, God smiled and answered:

*'True, man's sole property is the moment's time he lives;*
*Everything he fights for, stays here!'*

The man dozed off in silent submission.

# LOVE

# WANTED TO SING
# FOR YOU

Wanted to sing for you,
But the tune of your choice is not fine-tuned;
Wanted to dance for you,
But the rhythm of your choice has multiple beats;
Wanted to walk with you,
But your journey has no definite destination;
Wanted to dine with you,
But your heterogeneous company deflates appetite;
Wanted to dwell in you,
But you have improvised your castle into
A distillation gadget for excretory products
Of heterogeneous organisms!

Tell me,
Does a name rhyme with a career?
Does Dinnah mean diving for every Dick and Donne?
Does being a Rovance compel you to roam all over?
Do the Ritahs have to litter themselves?

Wish the Diana's denounced their surveyor-ship instinct, and
Received a song of lasting melody.

# OF MODERN FRIENDSHIP

Once friends always friends;
I shall commit myself to you as long as:
You do not drift into poverty,
Your good connections land me into property and power.

Shower me with praises;
Starve me of criticisms,
Thwart my foes,
Cheer my friends,
Never mind even if it harms your fortunes;
Never bother me with your misfortunes;
Our friendship shall entertain my own problems;
Our friendship is never about your problems.
Remember your secrets are ours, mine are mine!

# EASY COME, EASY GO

Your instant yes ignited yelps of disbelief,
The flooding of vastness of your versatile designs
evaporated my disbelief.
Generous elevations from
Dear to Darling,
Sweetheart to Honey to Angel,
Mauled me into ecstatic madness,
In reciprocity, I madly flung mud at my mild former!

My Millennium love-drainer, I thank you.
You're a moralist who reminded me:
Vastness means no versatility,
Vestine means no Valentine!
Easy come, Easy go.

Your magnetic caress cheered me mad,
Your flashy stay flung me into mud.

# I NEED WEDDING RINGS

For reasons you know better,
I beg to propose a multiple of rings.
My current ring is handicapped, it neither
ring-fences jealous,
curtails compulsory respect, nor
demarcates non- sharable dimensions.

I need a ring for fingers, not a finger,
A co-joined pair for the eyes;
two more co-joined pairs for the limbs; and
two dozen, each for the multiple dimensions of the heart and mind.
Rings whose life span is longer than the bearer's.

Human beings, being multi-dimensional and dynamic;
One ring, and forever is a sea of over-simplification.

# NATURE
# &
# SOCIETY

# THE SONG OF AGE

Am neither human nor a spirit but situation,
I visit everybody without an invitation card,
Am time-driven but no device can drive me in reverse.
Human beings both love and hate me!
Parents pray entreating me to visit their children,
They spring into song.
The very parents pray to have more of me
But none of my manifestations on them!

My name is Age,
No man can curtail my craft:
I crump succulent faces into dry rags;
String tight skin falls off-bones at sixty.
I smash rock-hard white teeth into
grey rotten maize seeds,
I suckle ball bouncing breasts into
Thread-bear pair of socks;
I replace lovers with sympathizers;
I dress jaws with teeth and pluck
The same jaws naked at seventy;
I crack a spring back into
A loose bow string;
I replace hope with worries about tomorrow.
Am an elusive thief;
I outwit satellite security details;
I out-maneuver money and might into palaces.

# PERHAPS, HEAVEN KNOWS
# WHAT GOES AMISS

*Recollections About My Father*
*Through Four Decades Effective Thirties*

Heaven knows what goes amiss, perhaps!
As if sixty-six cramps thirty-three into a sugar cane cramp.

At eleven,
My daddy was thirty-three,

At twenty- two he clocked forty-four,
He made fifty-five as I ticked thirty-three,
He piled sixty-six as I filed forty-four, and
I trail him forth.

Nonetheless, my memory taunts,
The sight dazzles my eyes,
The bitter reality slits my hope.
The lightening swift strides of thirty-three
Have handed-over to the sluggish steps of sixty-six,
The sluggishness that relentlessly beckons snail crawls.

The summer morning star forehead that
Splashed dazzling midday sunrays, that was,
Is now, but an extinguished flame of a winter haze!
The chlorophyll saturated, green, due dripping leaf, is now
A variegated withering tissue in the Sahara!
Blunt appetite and chilled ambition
Consumed the Napoleonic zeal to conquer the world.

# THEY WONDERED WHY!

A one-time Beauty Queen wondered why
men no longer swarmed her,
Men told her that time had eroded her treasure!

An emeritus ruler wondered why
crowds no longer showered him with cheers,
Countrymen told him that that was then!

An insolvent tycoon wondered where
beggars went,
Mockers told him that time had elevated most of
them to billionaires!

Then the trio wondered if beauty, glory and fortune are a mockery,
or if people are mockers.
The answer was 'nay'-
Beauty, glory and fortune are real, people are
no mockers either:
The only mocker of mankind is time!

# DEATH
# &
# METAPHYSICS

# DEATH, TELL ME

*In Memoriam of Yorokamu Turyomunsi, Our Distant Cousin.*
*He Died in A Fire Accident at Busitenia University in July 2012.*

Why do we run from you to you?
Yorokamu ran from fire and rammed into a spear!
Death tell me:
Whose disciple, are you?
God's?
Or Satan's?
What of your inspiration?
Sinner's punishment?
Or the righteous' retirement?

Death, you are the wonder of wonders,
Your ever- elastic stomach,
Your omnivorous nature,
Your gigantic appetite,
Your notion of justice,
Your insurmountable power,
All a marvel to man's imagination:
Your stomach stomachs the cactus and venomous scorpions

~

You lower Kilimanjaro height elephants, and
Only heaven knows how the same cheek contracts
to munch mud-fish!

Death, tell me your source of might,
The might that conquers the mighty,
What of the mystery of your magic?
The magic that levels ranks:
You know no money, and respect no ranks,
Your command coils the crafty,
Your wave devours dictators,
Your pronouncement silences professors,
You never mind bereaving the bereaved of their beloved!
You force foes into the same train,
Warlords into the same passage with captives,
Queens in the same queue with maids,
Landlords along with tenants!
Shall we say, maybe, you are a leveler?

Death, tell me your model of justice:
Why prefer saints to sinners?
Why select lone child, and spare dozens
Why teenagers instead of their great grand's?
Why bereave orphans of their lone bread-winner?

Are you an identical twin with love?
Love is blind of class, character, and creed;
You are blind of love, aspiration, and deed;
And both of you know no age limit!

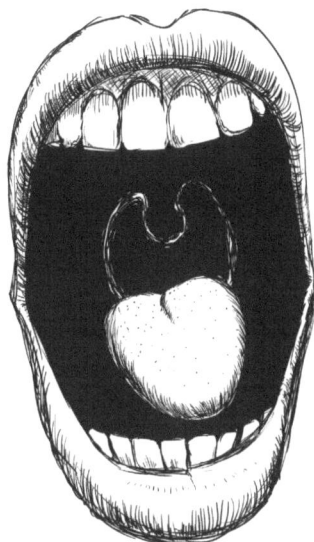

# THE INSATIABLE GULLET

*In Memoriam of Alex A. Kamujuni Ruraza, RIP,*
*Who Died in A Road Accident April 2004.*

Perhaps police never keep a record,
No matter though, you have not forgotten:
The four Daily Monitor journalists at Nakawa-Kyambogo,
Sixty students at Rwentanga in a School truck,
Seventy at Rutooto aboard S.B coach,
The Kigali-Kampala bound Jaguar at Kyogo
that silenced sixty in a second!
Will the Isingiro voters ever forget Hon Chaka?
Will the Budiope voters ever forget Hon. Henry Balikowa?
What of Professor Mujaju of Makerere University?
Tell me, have you forgotten Harman Basudde?
What of Bryan Bukenya? So young a brain!
What of Francis Ayume?
The once star Speaker of Parliament and Attorney General
Smitten on the slippery passage, too!

As of numbers, even Isaac Newton wouldn't accurately count!
Yet insatiable.
You many not mind the bereavement, the brains robbed of us.
But tell me the difference -
Is it the diving driver or the dime-happy traffic officer?
The gullied gullet, rather glutton?
Or the triple loaded vessels?
Maybe, the dent decorated road knows better!
The road ever unloading herself,
A brain drainer of sorts,
Specialist in reaping unripe fruits, and
An agent of liquidation!
Whatever, be kind and visit Kigali for a lecture, if
The speed-governor is out of stock.

# GOODBYE 2012,
# BYE-BYE DORCUS

*In Memory of Dorcus Our Youngest Sister Who Passed On,*
*December 28th, 2012. She Was Only Twenty-One.*

Time cuts a more divine, mystic form than us,
It was there, it will ever be
But it is ever sliding into darkness, too.
Be it bad or good times,
Angelic or devilish people,
Lordship or Serfdom,
Joy and Sorrow,
Nothing lives forever, everything is nothing!

All the year down the road,
*Maawe* and *Taata* pleaded with the Stars;
*Richard* and *Peninah* gave their all,
All of us as she saw, and knows
Tried whatever we could but
Fate mocked our vain effort!
Drenched in tears as 2012 sunk,
Our empty beings hanging on numb shells, and

Our minds rendered vacant,
We vacantly watched our Dorcus slide into oblivion
Where she joined a bigger family,
And patiently waiting for us, one by one.

Bye-bye Dorcus,
We will soon join you
As you joined them into that
Dreaded sacred planet.

# ABOUT MUGUMYA AMOOTI, R

Mugumya Amooti, R is a Ugandan poet, short story writer, novelist and author of school books. He has lived and worked in Rwanda for almost a decade. Due to this fact, some of his works are set in Rwanda. His novella, The Princess of Kigali is among such works.

Before joining Master Research Media, ltd as a Managing Editor, Mr. Mugumya lectured Literature in English and Communication Skills across universities in East Africa for a decade.

"The Trumpet and Other Poems from East Africa" is his third collection. It follows "The Song of Tobacco and Other Poems" and "The Song of War and Other Poems". Before the end of next year, he expects to complete "The Minister's Menu and Other Poems".

To-date, he is a visiting Quality Assurer for English language with Rwanda Education Board. Mr. Mugumya also participated in the 2018 African Writers Fellowship.

www.ingramcontent.com/pod-product-compliance
Lightning Source LLC
LaVergne TN
LVHW010025070426
835509LV00001B/20